Autumn's Yard

poems by

Anne Averyt

Finishing Line Press
Georgetown, Kentucky

Autumn's Yard

Copyright © 2016 by Anne Averyt
ISBN 978-1-63534-047-1 First Edition
All rights reserved under International and Pan-American Copyright Conventions. No part of this book may be reproduced in any manner whatsoever without written permission from the publisher, except in the case of brief quotations embodied in critical articles and reviews.

ACKNOWLEDGMENTS

My thanks to the editors of these publications in which poems appeared, sometimes in earlier form.

Best of the Burlington Writers Workshop 2014: counting emptiness
580 Split: Trust
Third Wednesday: Tabled Touch
RiverLit: Summer Pining
Best of Burlington Writers Workshop 2015: ever bloom
Dear Sister: Letters from Survivors of Sexual Violence: Hike to Again

Publisher: Leah Maines

Editor: Christen Kincaid

Cover Art: Anne Averyt

Author Photo: Alan Averyt

Cover Design: Elizabeth Maines

Printed in the USA on acid-free paper.
Order online: www.finishinglinepress.com
   also available on amazon.com

Author inquiries and mail orders:
Finishing Line Press
P. O. Box 1626
Georgetown, Kentucky 40324
U. S. A.

Table of Contents

When green no longer sways 1
Turning 70 3
Whooo 4
autumn afternoon 5
questioning night 6
Fall Leaves 7
Passing Thoughts 8
Giving Way 10
Circe Song 12
Questing Immortality 13
first light 14
Sur le Pont des Arts 15
night swell 16
counting emptiness 17
Trust 18
Tabled Touch 19
speech less 20
words 21
Leap the Dips 22
Hike to Again 23
Where is the Love ? 24
Green Hope 25
Summer Pining 26
ever bloom 27
Self Reflection 28
Musk of Memory 29
Going home 30

"For what is a poem but a hazardous attempt at self-understanding"

Robert Penn Warren

When green no longer sways

Gone the birds
before the leaves
their home felled
by chain and saw
though in the orchard
apples hang round
ripe with welcome

Distant in the yard
wind whips the maples
lifts their skirts
to dance and sway
life still full
in verdant morn

Here the doves in coo
mourn their loss
of spindly perch
the blight that ate
the evergreens
vacates rest
for chickadees

Gone the nuthatch
gone the jay
no more a spreading branch
for wrens to pause
or wormwood
for a downy feast

Amidst this stretch
of new expanse
I sit listening
to the memory
of evening owls
the racing swish
of fork-tailed swallows
staccato rap-tap-tap
of redheaded thrummers

Pining the emptiness
of autumn's yard
when green no longer
sways in singing wind
and shadows do not dance
in lingering light

When all that remains
to fill evening's sky
is the silhouette
of geese
turning

Turning 70

Queen Anne laces
the field
black-eyed Susans
splash color
standing tall
in the company
of thistles
hollow reeds sway
in a sea of green
late summer's legacy
urging me
shake loose
the cloak of dreams
that nestle night
open wide
the drape of day
walk dew deep
through meadow grass
join the rat-tat-tat
of the woodpecker's feast
before twilight
chills August
into memory
and distant
stars open

Whooo

The owl is gone
the whooo
of early morn
I drink my coffee
first arising
look beyond
wonder
what will
I do today

No one needs
my help
to pick them up
answer why
blow a kiss
goodbye

Autumn falls
green seeping
to yellow
ruby to rust
sunlight ceases dawdling
chill dances up
my spine

Fresh from summer sleep
winter stirs white
waiting for me
to print upon
a story song a step
where none has been
giving time
for the owl
to circle home
singing whooo
new am I?

autumn afternoon

sun golden the leaf
lets go its branch perch
nestles into rust
curls to crimson

breeze a sway
pine needles light
shadow dappled
beneath an evergreen

gazing in prickle grass
I sit longer now
than when
years passed

too busy
life rushed
too late
treasuring

the sun splash
wonder of time
suspended
in a leaf fall

questioning night

death hovers
my shoulder
time stirs
rest less
questioning
is it all
I thought
worth
reaching
the stretch
of my grasp
the crown
of my stars
or softness
in touch
grace full
in heart

Fall Leaves

On this morning of tomorrow I step into autumn where reds bleed and yellows shout, the edges of life sharp, passion fruit no longer sweet. I must think now of where I want to go, not think of snows to come, when fingers will no longer move and heart beat out of sync. In the garden I linger, smelling yesterday's honeysuckle, watching the ragged alphabet of geese spell goodbye, not knowing it would come to this, that lines would grow deep, eyes dim and children belong to children. Will I soon walk on three legs, lose by lunch the memory of morning tea? Not yet ... In this moment I will stand tall as running green leaves behind the color wheel. In this moment, I will count the silver in my hair and the gold in my teeth and know I am rich.

Passing Thoughts

Cats come home to die
in a hidden space
dark and comforting
my grandfather says
he wants to come home to die
not linger in a hospital
surrounded by strangers
who read his name
from a chart

I want to find the cat
wrap him softly
in a blanket
stroke his head
but he wants
to be alone
to slip away

My grandfather never
got his wish
he died tethered
to a metal bed
so he wouldn't fall

The cat dies curled
beneath my bed
I'll bury him
in the yard
by twilight

My grandfather rests
in pine repose
while reflected on a screen
his life passes
my nephew strumming
Amazing Grace

I stand silent
in the corner
hidden like the cat
at eventide
wondering

When time passes
will they find me
unbound
by the bed

Giving Way

We've gathered
to give away his life
the cups and chipped plates
the ones not too badly damaged
go to Salvation.

The chest that held a lifetime
of old letters amidst
the underwear
has been claimed
by his nephew.

Our cousin spoke for the empire
chair in the living room
of this house
where no one lives
anymore.

In the pantry the aunts
are carrying away
the spoils, doling out
the remains.

In the entry someone
has taken time
removed the clock
from the wall
and pocketed the key.

The house will be emptied
of possessions
no one wants
then sold
to the highest bidder.

The problem is
what to do
with his soul
mate Lucky
the retriever.

No one wants him
but it's a shame
to put him down
just because
his master
is gone.

All the questions
no one asks
all the memories
no one wants
fill the house
we are emptying
cup by cup
as if it were easy
giving way.

Circe Song

What is it like to drift alone
in space seeking the god particle
of matter making?

If I step 10 billion years will I see
space playing catch with universes,
find a pattern swirling chaos ?

Where will I land, who will I meet
out there beyond one small step,
one giant leap?

Questing Immortality

Is there a place souls go
beyond cloud swept skies
deep in swirling space
that holds the spirit

A soul space older
than plunging canyons
carved by ice flowing inward
deeper than the ocean bed
where undisturbed
crustaceans sleep

Time past I had no care
to ponder but sitting now
beneath a twilight dome
I wonder if somewhere
a gathering of spirit
tenders the solace
of eternity

first light

the fog walks
in early
morning
wraps its arms
in dew embrace
the budded rose
breathes prickled scent
daffodils droop
petunias plead
pinching
arising the sun
splits the mist
splays open
morning's
yearning

Sur le Pont des Arts

Star light dances
the Seine
glistens
love locks
hanging
on the bridge
whispers to day
a soft farewell

Suspended
two lovers kiss
deep into the night
stirring in me
the ache of long ago
the memory
of our love
new and fierce

When night held
the promise
of forever
and we kissed full
beneath
a ripened moon
love locked
sur le Pont des Arts

night swell

I drift
through night
tunneling dreams
hours moan
shadows pace

Stirring I reach for you
across a white divide
phantoms touch
morning
still

counting emptiness

I try not to count
emptiness
hoping love
like loaves
will multiply
fish will leap
to feast
ten thousand
and I will
scrabble time
hold more
than air
breathe
more
than
memory
find fullness deep
inside
the hollow
of your arms

Trust

I want to reach out
and touch someone
hold hands and know
we are together

But what if I reach out
and find all there is
to clutch is air
vanishing

Tabled Touch

It's 4 am, I read a poem
    by Katherine Mansfield
about sharing chamomile tea
    at night with him
across the table, in the kitchen
    knees touching

I feel the ache of a limb
    no longer there
except in memory, pain
    phantomed real

Easy to slip
    in the shadows
missing a limb, hard
    to retrace your steps
find where you stored
    your hope

My leg running fast
    through the night, me
in pursuit trying to catch it
    so I have something to feel
when at night I sit in the kitchen
    with tea

speech less

listen to the quiet
the poet said
before you speak
to paper
reach to the silence
torrenting inside

needing more
than words
to say come
let's dance
the years

holding
the touch
of his eyes
the tilt of his head
his laughter tumbling
knowing the taste
of his breath
the soul of his heel

now left only
with the pierce
of emptiness
bellowing
in the silence
that comes
before words

words

were all
I had left
when he left
words and history
the carved mantel dragons
from Cambodia
painted Delft plates
souvenir of his
Amsterdam trip
the two headed
cyan raku pot
and pictures
abandoned
the carnivorous bed
mismatched
wedding china
the Bose speakers
that played
our songs

now words
haunt my nights
words chase me
down the hall
soul howling words
broken words
split sentences
struggling
for sense
sated words
that will not stop
until I cry
free

Leap the Dips

The divorce is history, my life in double figures. I leap for joy like when I won at hopscotch or first rode my bike alone; my father let go and I held my balance, forgetting I didn't know how. This spring I joined the circus, learned to walk a tightrope holding only the pole of myself, learned to fly through the air and be my own safety net. Now I can walk on hot coals, I can be cut in half and still be whole. I am my own clown launched from a cannon to find my own way. Like a child I line up for cotton candy and sweet caramel apples. For the first time I ride the roller coaster, leap the dips, and in the end still have my stomach.

Hike To Again

Soul weary I look to the mountain
smell the energy of conquest
hear birds in meadow sing
of moving on ...

        Ripple of water
      coming back upon itself
  whispering more
    whispering reach

I breathe in the cold air
stretch taut muscles
I forgot I had
my heart
calling

      Go on ... Climb
    Learn to love again
and I whisper *Now*
  and fly away

Where Is the Love ?

We're orphans now, my sister says,
adult orphans, meaning we always were
only now it's official.

She was a good mother, my brother tries,
she kept us fed and clothed ... and
the house was always clean.

Standing there by her still
on a railed bed, he speaks
for all of us, the orphans.

What he cannot speak cries
Where is the love? Long ago
a pop song, the needle stuck ...

Where is the love? We are afraid to ask,
where the warm embrace, the smile softly
saying *You are the sunlight of my soul.*

Our eyes reach, our hands fall, hearts emptied ...
Does anyone know, do they adopt orphans
bending on wounded knees ?

Does anyone know ... *Where is the Love?*

Green Hope

earth opened
to swallow
her boxed remains
five summers gone
and still I sit
in memory
unable
to rise
free
touch the lining
of unfettered self
find in sunlight
a clover's petal
whispering hope
promising *yes*
she loves me
she loves me not
she loves me

Summer Pining

The pines in my backyard thrive
surviving summer's heat
healing from the blight
that took down a sister
stump sawed to the ground

Now I see clearly the cars
circling the roundabout, sound
no longer muffled, green gone
to gray metal and oval eyes
no where for crows to nest
or squirrels climb

I turn my chair to look beyond
where standing still
two orphan pines
reach skyward
touching blue
while in my heart

The ache remains
of mother gone
sleeping
in a distant land
beneath a weeping maple
head resting on earth
in a row of strangers

Where I will never go
letting someone else
tend the land
pull the weeds
protect the
memory

ever bloom

rapt in the rose bush
twined in beauty
you pretend
thorns don't rip
skin loose
prickle blood
on the soft scent
of pink

hope in a blossom
you see
but not me
trapped a moth
in a bell jar
pockets stone filled
heart darkened
wading river deep

breathing fragrant afternoon
you snip a bouquet
celebrate *yes yes*
a thousand times
but forget me
here alone
deep inside
weeping
earth

Self Reflection

The ghosts of time write on my mirror, tell me how to see myself alone, love a smudge of lipstick cornering my smile, hair wisped thin and rooted gray. Is this me, folds around the waist, lines carved while I slept? I stepped into the looking glass young and full of hope, who is this now reflecting back at me? This morning of yesterday I had no need of putting on a face, hiding time from passersby. This morning of now the mirror cracks the fragile shell of who I think I am, tells me where I have been but keeps the secret of tomorrow when I will have no need of questioning, of looking in the mirror to know who once I was, who I am now and who will be remembered when breath no longer fogs the mirror in the hall.

Musk of memory

the distant sycamore
will still bend
in breeze
the pine left
alone
will still rise
stately
to touch the moon
journeying full
in night sky

without alarm
mourning doves
nest still
in brittle branch
mocking birds chatter
squirrels scuttle
not knowing
saw and chain
will soon strip
the yard
of majesty
open wide
a meadow view

pining this new expanse
of emptiness
I sway in memory
breathe the passing musk
grieving less
wanting more
still rooted
in earth
bending

Going Home

The waves wash the shore
then run away without
looking back

Anne Averyt's romance with words has been lifelong. Her journalism career spans fifty years and four states. But it is through poetry that Averyt finds her authentic voice. Using sparse language and evocative imagery, Averyt's poetry seeks to "capture a moment, share an emotion, contemplate a thought."

"My first love was a priest ... and a poet," Averyt says. "Gerard Manley Hopkins captured my heart and imagination through his love of words, how he used them to paint landscapes and explore soulscapes. I, too, want my poetry to touch my readers, to disquiet and to comfort. I'm not a priest, but I love being a poet."

Anne Averyt is author/co-author of books published by Random House and EP Dutton. Currently, she facilitates groups on a mental health crisis intervention unit in her hometown of Burlington, VT and is a Commentator on Vermont Public Radio. Her work has appeared in journals including *580 split, Third Wednesday, Riverlit, the Aurorean,* and *Best of Burlington Writers Workshop, 2013, 2014, 2015.*

www.ingramcontent.com/pod-product-compliance
Lightning Source LLC
LaVergne TN
LVHW041506070426
835507LV00012B/1355

9781635340471